AutoPortrait

(as flotsam)

Recent and Selected Titles from Tupelo Press

Song in Tammuz
Avia Tadmor

Blue Selvage
Preeti Parikh

of Women: 20 Japanese Female Poets / 20 Waka Poems
Naoko Fujimoto

Them That Slept: New and Selected Poems
Larissa Szporluk

Other Paths for Shahrazad
Jennifer Jean, ed.

Slipstream
Diana Cao

The Book of Marys and Glaciers
Carrie Olivia Adams

The Andrew Wyeth Chronicles
Janée Baugher

Identifying the Pathogen
Jennifer Militello

Indifferent Cities
Ángel García

Something Small of How to See a River
Teresa Dzieglewicz

Force Drift: An Essay in the Epic
Jeffrey Pethybridge

Tips to Help You Do Your Best
Mike Carlson

Cyborg Fever
Laurie Sheck

Daphne
Kristen Case

Nebulous Vertigo
Belle Ling

Westminster West
Chard de Niord

Jalousie
Allyson Paty

Mycocosmic
Lesley Wheeler

Phantom Number: An Abecedarium for April
Spring Ulmer

The Haunting
Cate Peebles

The Radiant
Lise Goett

The Opening Ritual
G.C. Waldrep

The Right Hand
Christina Pugh

Called Back
Rosa Lane

Landsickness
Leigh Lucas

Green Island
Liz Countryman

The Beautiful Immunity
Karen An-hwei Lee

Small Altars
Justin Gardiner

Country Songs for Alice
Emma Binder

Asterism
Ae Hee Lee

then telling be the antidote
Xiao Yue Shan

Therapon
Bruce Bond & Dan Beachy-Quick

membery
Preeti Kaur Rajpal

How To Live
Kelle Groom

Sleep Tight Satellite
Carol Guess

THINE
Kate Partridge

The Future Will Call You Something Else
Natasha Sajé

Night Logic
Matthew Gellman

The Unreal City
Mike Lala

Wind—Mountain—Oak: Poems of Sappho
Dan Beachy-Quick

Tender Machines
J. Mae Barizo

Best of Tupelo Quarterly
Kristina Marie Darling, ed.

We Are Changed to Deer at the Broken Place
Kelly Weber

Why Misread a Cloud
Emily Carlson

The Strings Are Lightning and Hold You In
Chee Brossy

Ore Choir: The Lava on Iceland
Katy Didden and Kevin Tsang

The Air in the Air Behind It
Brandon Rushton

AutoPortrait (as flotsam)

KIRSTEN KASCHOCK

T|P

Tupelo Press
North Adams, Massachusetts

AutoPortrait (as flotsam)

Library of Congress Control Number:2026939722

ISBN: 978-1-961209-68-8 (paper), 978-1-961209-74-9 (eBook)

Cover and text design by Josef Beery.

Cover art: Kirsten Kaschock

This publication of this book is made possible in part through a generous grant from an anonymous Tupelo Press angel.

First paperback edition September 2026

Tupelo Press
P.O. Box 1767
North Adams, Massachusetts 01247
(413) 664-9611 / Fax: (413) 664-9711
editor@tupelopress.org / www.tupelopress.org

Tupelo Press is an award-winning independent literary press that publishes fine fiction, non-fiction, and poetry in books that are a joy to hold as well as read. Tupelo Press is a registered 501(c)(3) nonprofit organization, and we rely on public support to carry out our mission of publishing extraordinary work that may be outside the realm of the large commercial publishers. Financial donations are welcome and are tax deductible.

Acknowledgments

Selections from this manuscript (sometimes in different versions) have been published or accepted for publication in the following publications:

American Poetry Review
The Arts Fuse
Bennington Review
New Orleans Review
Poetry Magazine
A Public Space
Your Impossible Voice

Form was not born from an idea.
It was an idea vanishing.
— Cecilia Vicuña

Table of Contents

III.

Nomad
(star)

On the outskirts of every agony sits some observant fellow who points.

—Virginia Woolf

paints

I cannot be the only one who recalls the quality of light more clearly than the plot of things.

I.

maiden
(woman)

Arearea no varua ino

Do not finish your work too much.

It leads to death. When you perfect
a field, a field cannot breathe. If you touch her
ceaselessly, she will numb to what is
soft. I say withhold the fruit until the table
ripens. I have seen a child wither and rot
from too much getting. Sit at back of hut
and train your eyes to drink. Given time, colors
may accept you as vessel, ferment. Draw them
out—luxuriate in fume. Every stroke
has an origin. A terrible seed. These are mock
oranges, unfit to taste. Except. Give in utterly
to the work and find that everything has happened.
Rimbaud, for example. Leave. Have your long life.
Outlive your children even as you peruse
others'. The world is books. Your hands may be
starved for its pages but driftwood—by sea polished
to bone—stays jagged where God has broken
the femur. The missionary's promise. In lieu of
mansion, erect lean-tos on beaches you dreamt
into existence as though they weren't already there.
Any pleasure that lives lives in its endless washing
away, how far sin drifts beyond a girl's hurt
before ocean returns it, ground to fine volcanic
pitch. Art you do not conclude, it is what it will become,
however unlikely. It cannot be helped.

(Paul Gauguin)

Never a Humbert nor a Lolita be.

At twelve I did not imagine I could be assumed seductive.

Letters were sent things I thought disclosed the soul. At fourteen I was a sophomore (or less). He'd graduated college. I lived on a crick, him a big lake. Michigan—a sneeze caught in the throat.
Suppressed.

Bodies of water figure largely in my *thos*, a deletion-mutation of *thesis*, ciphery *o* replacing three letters, three dots of ellipsis, three steps down.

My *thos* is this: It was near impossible, before selfies, for a girl to be her own muse (omissions litter graveyards with woodmen) and this may explain what is perceived as a willingness to participate in one's commodification.

Draw me. See me. Make me real.

Lolita is a retelling of Pinocchio, carved from beach-starved driftwood. But in this respeak everyone else is lying, and so she shrinks—the girl—into woman, just there, at the end. An uninteresting woman. No longer a-mused. Strings cut, sadly aging, not gilded . . . childed, and thus a child no longer

: hinges all unned.

At this point I could mention I married a geneticist. Or is "deletion mutation" enough? Does the fact that I was a serial academic explain this desire to show my work?

Make no mistake, mistakes are work.

I don't want to show it per se. Vivisect it maybe. I am fascinated by how making happens, minds recombining information in the service of novel offspring.

The geneticist and I have three almost-grown sons.

A fortune teller at Coney Island counted out my pregnancies by withholding her thumb. Oppositional hitchhiking. I took this as destination, self: *You will go nowhere with a stranger.*

I grew up staring into mirrors but had no luck in reading that girl there. She was disagreeable.

To be blunt—she never agreed with me.

Well Baby Clinic

If it kills you, you've gone too far.

The sea, I mean. If you walk out into
its maw without thought, you will die.
I don't care what kind
of swimmer you are—and it's the same
with children. I was one, then
had one. What else to do? There's too much
pain for mastery, but it does make the work
better. It makes the self more evident
in the work when you're gulped-down
breastmilk in other spheres. That's how
tits get to be like eyes. Downcast.
It's not there's not
great joy in being
consumed. And of course the pleasure.
For example: I like a fried plantain
on occasion, the sweet and fat,
the salt of it. Babies can be like that
—managing to live. Later tastes evolve, pigment
pools into bruised cloud. You see the
fingerprints there? That's holding become
shaking, love unvarnished. There be
oceans in the skies ready to pull you
dry. And all the ones you were
assured would survive this place—
its greedy mouths—they keep looking black.

(Alice Neel)

I can say it now. My abortion. I have practiced saying it, in French—*m'abortion*. It is a thing my mother never said to my father, a kept thing.

So he would not be ashamed. Because she was.

My mother had her children. All of them, then others'. She believes it a virtue: playing the hand dealt. Certainly she had already left the church. Things we don't leave marks.

A litany vows to say and say. I have asylums of m'mory: Kubla Khan, Carrion Comfort, Casabianca. Some sonnets. Stanzas. Jabberwocky.

No daughterets.

How many lines would they have? How many syllables? Vorpal swords? I will not know.

Eventually sorrows swallowed find their frequency—their color, meter, rhyme: first bled, then let.You might call such a form Echo. It could reproduce only what was done to it, or less.

No.9 (Dark over Light Earth)

One day the black will swallow the red.

I am not thinking *[sic]* of a brick wall. I am
not *[sic]* drawing here death but only a crow
with a berry, the wrong berry. A *[sic]*k crow
who cannot feed its young or its parents'
other young or the young of its siblings
when Windshield hits Sister, hurtling as it has
through the middle-distance too far
above Road, some trailer's tractor
come through that shouldn't've, not
early hours, not this shunpike. Drivers do
though. They search out detours as I—artist—
make doom concrete in doomed efforts
to avoid it. I know of no way to
carve Shangri-la from asphalt. Nevertheless
I carry a shovel. Taken for a gravedigger, I
guffaw, tell stories of the dead
so they think they are
correct—the dead. They mistake me.
Knowing what you see when you see it
is its own brand of obscenity. I have thoughts
I tuck away too, like translucent beads of rice.
Thousands of birds each year find them-
selves dead from weddings. The whole thing
hurts (four-darks-in-red). I won't be tied to bed-
posts of the literal or lashed to some bloodied

orange bridge. Drop one stone from there
and the ocean rises like yeast off sunset. One
glacier—melted—goes in and on, as if
anyone had never been alone.

(Mark Rothko)

When I first sat down on a bench in front of one and saw it breathing at the edges it felt a little like tripping.

That was an illusion. I hadn't that day.

For long minutes I looked, let what I saw steep in the cracked cup of me. But I did it—partly experiencing, partly watching myself experience.

I'd seen his work before on postcards, on posters.

In the flesh, the canvas felt more like skin. Like it could blush, like it pulsed.

In spite of their bodies, I have not ever loved them, Rothko's paintings. As I have no desire to visit his black chapel. To be inside of that. Texas.

I've seen photographs. I feel as if I know how it would be among viscera disguised as chalkboard. Knotted, charred. No language left, not in most obscuring cloud, burningest bush. Isn't that the antithesis of religion?

Anthos: school like an organ, its liverful of mute children.

The dark, flowering.

At college I'd museum, quick-skipping through gallery into sculpture garden: a stone place to be. On East Rock, for example, I'd sit on an overhang, legs overhanging. In the distance the sound glinted. Graphite.

I tried here and there to comprehend time but could not fit my arms around.

My childhood held little silence. Books were boulders—loud, interrupting the water, collapsing hours upon the self in a vanishing act.

A roommate introduced me to Rothko. Dead as books I thought. I met them both years later, again for a first time. In the interim she'd inhabited silence as pre-nun, a Buddhist novitiate for eighteen months before deciding against.

I found this nearly unfathomable. She must've learned things about breath.

One October I took my boys to visit her. We picked heirloom apples in the mist. We drank cold water out of mason jars, the maple trees a week past peak red, wind bringing leaves down in volume.

Volume is a measurement of space. Rivers of leaves, soundsful.

So it is with the empty air in a museum. It keeps touching the paintings, and the guards either do not notice or have learned not to say.

Tree Roots

No. He studies a single blade of grass.

My own mind lies low, looking to
men whose whole lives they've lost too
to looking. Do not think me circular. I'm no dog
spiraling into nest. Plus, I cannot by any means
sleep. Color is to blame. It will not be
arrested. Me, I shall die.
There is only the matter of manner.
Ends require discrete methodologies, forms breed
functions no scientist predicts. No man—none
—can claim honestly to be *of science*. He does
not know. But I do. It is a weight I carry
in my palette. Thus I am no man
and the resulting exile is both relief
and a keening. Imagine a rung bell: it grieves
because it is hollow. One is given only to sound
one's lack. If you climb the ladder of joy
towards a still life—think what cut stem means
to she who interrogated the flower, who scratched up
winter wood for the kiln. There is no art
for her, no bee she should catch in the melody
of her hair. Stung her whole body over, she is able
as *a bell*. Thus, the swelling. Children pour
out: crows from emptied field, having eaten, having
assumed. Green is not for long. Blue is a portal.

A blade of grass fails wielding. And yellow? It varies
as the light does: be it blinding or revelatory
—it is the stain of God.

(Vincent Van Gogh)

A troubling medium, portrait.

Its imbalanced trinities :

painter, sitter, painting ::
a coin (two faces, one rolling
edge) ::: angel/daemon/haint

But you can't pay your own way, can you? A patron then. And paint the porch.

Artists are kept things—a penny pressed for luck, etched locket chokered at jugular notch.

The lie is intimacy. Here, let me reveal a thing that is uncomfortable for us both, either your face or my deceit. Once made material, which one is immaterial.

And now you are supposed to trust me. Because we are so close—see?—my nose is burning at the tip. Like a clove.

Self-portraits are the most pitiless species of the form. Because of the immersion, the immolation. Imma tell you tho—it's not mirrors removing us from mercy.

Okay maybe it is.

Painting a self-portrait was once accomplished with a mirror—the looking glass incorporated, how the artist had to crane to encounter herself within gilt frame. See the glory of her neck?

Q: Who is Janus? Who is Narcissus? What fine line divides us?
A: Veni, vidi, vinculum.

And then there is the required devotion : milk-paint white, rose madder, or the palegreenblue of oceansky.

I think I would rather be / a painter, but I am not.

It were the most awful thing I could do—commit to a palette.

(Frank O'Hara)

Woman, Bird, Star

I closed myself within myself purposely.

The first method by which I tried to contain
miracles was to bind them to me with bandages.
I saw how the rest were living, under canary
yellow skies. But not light, it's things. A horse
causes shock, a pebble holds for an eon its motion
on inner walls. I've tried to move as boulders move
in gardens. Like gangrene. There's no arguing
with slow children or their guns. The way
I've employed the figure *bomb* is pure.
A symbolism, embolism. You'll want to spit out
my codex like Calder's wires, stabbing the air. Go
ahead. Akimbo me, all seven limbs. I've done the same
damaged spider outside the prison doors for years. Note:
hulkish planks do not divide so much as *promote*
division. War's countryside is heavier to enter even
than its churches. What do you know of
the fields outside the city? There, fruit is whole
and time cycles largely through triptychs. Spring bleeds
into summer's wounds. Smuggled from orchards
of the damned, the seeds and runes I've swallowed
sprout forth in ancient forms to claim the future.

(Joan Miro)

The book weaves. I say that. I say: dark thread, root and knot, thief. I don't knit. My mother-in-law crochets.

I say crow.

Cosmic threads cross the dense nothing. Someone out there is writing odes to absence like it's 1982.

On the day I met my mother-in-law, she brought out the christening gown she'd made for her son's firstborn. She did not know we were dating, we did not know we were dating, I was not Catholic, was not anything.

He didn't believe anymore but had informed no one. Of his tattoo. We hadn't, yet, had sex. Our delay was not religious, except my body was a temple—which did not mean Jewish or Mormon to my mother who told me what my body was. It meant vaguely Greek, or ancient. My childhood body already aged like hard cheese.

Dark thread, root and knot, thief: these I had scrawled across my skin. Don't boys piss in snow?

I'd long assumed my body's sacredness was suspect, since when she imparted the fact my mother's open hand was still flying—as the crows say.

AUTOPORTRAIT (AS FLOTSAM)

When sleep failed my early form, I sent its smallness beneath the bed.

To be flashlit, book calmed, box-sprung.

Anything but above.

Traffic would toss the upper room to carousel, walls become flickers. Day-colors ebbed, sucked back into grayscale. Thickened. The way water at night gets black, like blood is.

When I went under, I sometimes left my doll C. Josephine behind to take the sleep I couldn't. To sail away on a boat of mattress.

Because she mattered.

Other times I threw her against walls, twisted her limbs, bit and sucked on her hands.

I think I was painting.

II.

daemon
(bird)

Caryatid

The function of art is to struggle against obligation.

Someone wrapped the girl around a wasp—
around its cinch, she was circled
a dozen times or more, until wasp was un-
wasp, no longer able to wear wasp skirts
with the taut belt, even flying, even
stabbing compromised.
                                        It got so
bad—girl girding wasp in yo-yo—they had to
sit in perfect calm in the papercool hive having out
their ill-fit arrangement. "Why are you wound
this way?" went the universe (wasps refuse
the teleological) expecting a non-answer.
The girl tried to form a coherence
other than the shape leant her
by her strangling act.
                                    The thread
of things failed legibility, became a factless shriek
goring electric through the jam of her host's
ample abdomen, so that spasmed wasp just
made out "to bring you pain," and that
only. This, too, is how I am certain
a daughter would appear to me.
                                                    In plague.

(Amadeo Modigliani)

The Conodoguinet rose over the bank each March. After wet winters, it climbed the hill towards our yard. I never fished, never tubed down its winding towards Susquehanna, into Chesapeake, Atlantic, oblivion.

Insomnia: water shot through with trainsound from the yard in miles-off Enola, summer cicadas. Enola backwards is alone. Is me too. How I would.

Most dreamsongs are on their way elsewhere. My mother kept the windows open, no air-conditioning. The air, wild.

Alien husks clung to our screens.

In the spring of 1972, Lake Cayuga was readying to flood. The hurricane hit Florida on June 19th like a drunk, three days after my mother's labor/my birth, before climbing the coast. The following year the World Meteorological Organization retired her name like a baseball jersey: Agnes, not Agnus. No lamb, no god.

Stretching thirty-nine miles north to south, Lake Cayuga is the longest of the glacial Finger Lakes in New York, although not the middle lake, or finger. Ithaca, the town on its southern end, has a Greek name.

I gave the name Agnes to the protagonist of a novel I set in central Pennsylvania, not far from my childhood home and where the flood's damage was heaviest. My family moved from Ithaca when I was two. No odyssey, a simple car trip, straight down the map, the car blue.

The hurt one accrues living in certain locations can be gothic. Wet leaves, saplings sprouted from porch gutters, beauty drenched in apathy. Our house sat ten miles from Three Mile Island. During the meltdown, we were evacuated, briefly—the meltdown partial, a mere near-catastrophe seeding dread.

This was to be our next new state : loam for dread.

We came back home after two weeks spent in my father's sister's attic. What to believe—government or gut. My mother pregnant with one of my brothers. Almost the last of us.

Imagine, if you will, an ex-chemist returned to her family farm to breed a crow the size of a horse.

I have imagined that—her. Agnes.

Every fall after 1979 box elder bugs crept into our house like walking mold, their slow black bodies edged in red. My mother pinched them without ceremony from wall and sill.

Being small, we relish knowing the killings of which are capable.

It felt like punishment.

When she removed the books from my dancebag, I was seven, and she did it to encourage me. Between classes, I should make friends.

Books were sacred, a get-out-of-life-free pass.

I made friends. This fact does not change the essential quality of her actions but only makes my later judgement of it more complex.

Q: Now that books can be read without books, who will perform the essential thefts?
A: The unmothers.

I know this in their bones, being one.

Femur.

GRILLO

Medicine men live in caves.

You can see the comfort in that. Admitting
the loneliness, embracing the degree of
earth you crave around you, a burial
before the burial. You were once an intern.
You turned inward. You were interred.
It was the internet. Twitter was interminable.
Nothing ever ends, that is what the hole
in the darkness of the cave tells you, the fire
escaping. Commanded, you crawl up the out-
side of a tenement building to receive your ten
commandments and none of them suggests
scouring the oven, or why it's bad luck
to fall asleep with a burning stick dragging
from your teeth. You get tense. Don't
want to be a tenant in a life that doesn't
love you. You spend your terminal dollar
entering a terminal. You put on your tiara.
No one is there. No one wants you there.
You get to be old as fuck, cars jizz past.
No one reads anymore. Down below
the street is the only place you trust yourself
to see to the future. You sweep it clean
as a coal mine. There is nothing for it
but breaking. You fetch the new donkeys.

(Jean-Michel Basquiat)

My father is lessening. He has less memory, less vision. He has less hearing and less flesh, hair. What's there is white. His balance—lessened. He wobbles, has fallen. My father is not yet vanished. Thinning out, he prepares to pass, not through needle-eye but into next poem.

I need to listen harder. A boulder at ocean's edge.

When I left for college, he got a heart balloon. He lost a job, found a new one and talk radio. He won't admit this but I remember. Rush. We fought. I was a young woman, waxing. Swole.

It was my mother and I who battled when I was still a child, petite, forced thin. A single mint.

My father pushed me away and I bounced. My enlargement seemed silly and arrogant. Beach-ballish. My fury built no coherent structures for itself. I could not intricate my rage across in beast nor even form brute castles on the strand. I could fold no mounds of cloth, not worry clay.

Still, no knot is quite forgot.

On some withdrawing wave—its small bright blur.

Rage can be drawn as one face of god—though I think of no face, more doldrummed sea or silty low-tide delta, all of us mulch.

Should I not talk god? And yet the marketability.

Rage fuels action, and plots need action, don't they? Car chase, earthquake. Flood. (I never seem able to help myself.)

Bombs, bullets, drones. War. Truths are not pretty, they just are. Stars that do. Piercers disregarding any intervening flesh—*skeletons... able to walk on the wind.* I sometimes wish I could be neutral as an astrolabe. As analog.

I'd rather layer light than decipher it. This is maybe how an ocean acquires depths. In dance, to follow is not a single passive act but a series of recalibrations.

Decision not surrender.

To shape rage, I should observe then retrace its crouch and vault: in charcoal, in crow (that oldsky go-between), with bodies-made-instrument, with glitter and paste. All approximate.

The underworld is worlds. In one of them, art is neither echo nor cloying moon. Its shine immaculate—

its own disaster—having resisted all tyranny of star.

(Theo Jansen)

Brown Sun and Housetop

It is hard for a flat thing to understand a round one.

It would help if any of us understood language—if
asked to by the song of the word, we stood under, looked
up, made awe the condition of the day. Instead, we put
in place of the mystical, fixation. We overstand, circum-
stand.
            The shape of a boat is predicated on intelligence
of water. The bottom is crafted dome, is archway. Cathedral.
Drawl. It is called Long Island Sound so that we listen.
To live at the end of a long lake is to learn all ends
exist separately, just there, a length beyond
the long longed-for numb, its not un-
welcome frozenness.
                                        Always we are tasked with
succumbing. But a small life bound by shifting horizon
needn't blunt the mind. Modest portals want to open
between art and next. I have devoted myself to re-
formation: sense from abstraction. If we humble
ourselves before the slaughterhouse and accept
—yes, all mimesis reduces—we may yet get
how. How fidelity breeds lessness to
soften the kill, ask that we open
and turn away from theory
towards what is

                              simple, again, and new.

(Arthur Garfield Dove)

The idea of illuminating manuscripts, living a monk-life—this has been a shadow vessel for me. A sistership outskirting the recognized constellations. Me raising bees or living in a fifth-floor walk-up in Brooklyn. Without anyone but books.

My blue place. Where I don't live.

Lately I love, and so much about that love is so simple it makes everything else difficult.

Everything—the solitude I crave and am afraid of—I've given up to have it.

Like smoking. Like courting death (I don't/have children). How honey suffocates, petroleum, all the jellies. How cities blot out stars and bombs undo their buildings and pearl shoebuttons are crushed to glint and bonemeal.

Somewhere, giant's bread rises in a pewter bowl.

On the counter in another verse lays the threadbare dress of a disappeared doll—Charlotte. Charlotte Josephine. Her velvet coat brown as crust.

(You must expect fieldnotes
to be deranged. Ever needful of
ingathering. Mine anyway.)

AUTOPORTRAIT (AS FLOTSAM)

Once an aftermath is sown—green stakes claim where it shouldn't
and the nightsky becomes aurora, dank tome, apiary. Its yield?

: starsprout or dry mold or the senseless dribblings of daft and
grassy bee.

Ode to M'mory—

Sing a song of pixels / I don't have one, not as others do, don't quite
miss it / a vague throb alongside a hum of continuity / snapshot and
echo

of course I believe my past / lives—that night, *that year of now done /*
difference—I lived indifference

some other one is writing this / book, daubing my self-portrait dun

not a god, though maybe / a robot designed not-on-earth / welded
from perhaps scrap by some cosmic scamp

a scientist small-as-me / alchemistress mixing pigments until her
palette is dusty/blackboard or bird-like omen/—but rust-stiff
mechanical bird

: the poet twice-proxied

humans often mourn who they were before / the death rather
than the dead—as if / they could return their self to all selves once
emptied

as rivers do

these are flashes without/illumination they are like fireflies, insect-/
drones expiring in a jar losing/power, having long since lost the air

(Gerard Manley Hopkins)

SCIENCE AND CHARITY

Why not try to understand the song of a bird?

Could I reconsider context, sketch
carcass without scar—listen even?
The data speaks of one idea. Dying
of some other. Across the pleadings stream
yet another hue of tulle skirt overlaid
: net. The girl, ill. The girl dropped under
sheet, underwater. Is she in need
of medicine or dreams? This is a question
to pull from blossom. I have snatched
coins from that purse before. You
assume colors but no. Geometry.
I've stolen rival weaves of disk-
flower, sexed faces of orchid, and from
behind these—the irreducible numbers.
(Even I was once fifteen and feeling.)
Flatten figure into sky to ascertain
any frightened prey. You guess
ortolan, roasted. Now I can down
a feathered songbird whole, do not
doubt it. But consumption only mimics
comprehension. Better to unhinge, then
rearrange. Better to split—as they say
—the lark. My craft I've honed :
I rub with thumb, deseed the daisy.
I seek, I thieve, extract what lives
from what's inside the living.

(Pablo Picasso)

My sisters and I had no sanctioned nicknames. We were not religious, though our bodies felt somewhat holy, blessed by the rhythms of our pumping legs on swings vaulting us into high twilight.

Pennsylvania, New York, and Florida are swing states. You go away, you come back. I've never lived in Florida. I have lived in New York and Pennsylvania, Iowa and Georgia, and I've read Florida twice. But they were different books, by authors Schutt and Groff.

We are all different books.

A few months ago, a mateless crocodile produced a clutch of eggs. (This, on the internet.) In one, her keepers found a zoo Christ, perfectly formed but still as stone.

Clearly, this was a refusal.

A woman may be called a saint if she continues to reach up and out with her toes, nearly upside-down at her apex, for hours, despite those who'd follow her down the crick to the river and jump off the old railroad bridge would she simply play the piper. Candlewick.

Reader, she never does—any of it. Least of all lead.

Least of all, escape.

Ode to a Paperback—

Early Beatles sailing out the kitchen window over the four-foot
pool in the lower yard / sweat sealing me into woven plastic
lawnchair on our slab of patio / Dad searing burgers / *Please Please
Me* or *Love Me Do*?

I was eleven maybe / devouring the end of a book I wanted to
last/forever in the grip of its sci-fi climax / a girl proving capable
of herself

back-and-forth across the pool-aquarium my sister swam / a
dimpled fish / her translucent fingers wrinkled over its metal edge
in question mark

nothing as brief as late summer / stretches out so far beyond / itself
the smell of burning

The Architect

I have an assuredness of myself. I never protect myself against it.

I once frequented Utopia, the children's center. A life
can be built from the ground floor up, a recipe devised
from itch, scabbed up using at-hand ingredients. Dancing
dolls can stand stocking still among dark white ankles.
No one is certain whether they're seen how they were
intended or how they intend. Few lean in, fewer listen.
Color conveys its messages half-spelunked, unfully
swum. Sure clear strokes can beget wattage, can light
the lottery of a famed life. I once nearly retired
to rooms above the city where people go to drop
pretense. Beneath rockbottom. How people are fallen
then re-up is of grave interest to me (and quite possibly
beyond me). Prescriptions insist upon fulfilment. *Get up*
they say and so I paint them: the triangular people.
Triangular because they've legs they try to move
with. It seems purpose. That is how painting works.
How it codes its collisions. Offering a means for living
despite and surviving—by getting what cannot be
borne down to a more molecular construction.

(Jacob Lawrence)

Ode to a Mixtape—

On a great lawn at sixteen / roman candling at end of day / boombox
booming / *I am-I am Mandinka and I know what's happening*

barefoot in boxers / a dozen of us blowing off July steam in mad/
-dance mosh-pit stomp-flight

from all corners of the state kids / learning Arabic or Russian or
Japanese / all summer-longing Dov and me and Mary and Nandini / on
our own a first time before on our own / for good heaving languageless
angst / flinging rage and sweat and shame into the grass

for a few hours on a few days we do

we live

division is the first wound / how the light is slipped into separate
envelopes and cars drive away / in the exact shape and silhouette of
cars/into a second-hand dusk—its pink-and-gray erasing

and my sister (this is years before) she goes under

: echo of charcoal / chlorine shadow

(Sinead O'Connor, Michael Stipe)

"I will not live my life on repeat," my brother yells. (Not those exact words.) He falls into me. (We may not have touched.) I don't know who he's yelling at, but I nod. We've been looping since I was born on his island.

I think he might think I'm fey—never there quite, not letting him unlove me.

He's eager to hate, no one stopping him but him. It'd be easier to be unbothered by his miscalculus but I am not. I am bothered. Brothered.

There's plenty we've done, said, smoked. That was not our problem. We chased fireflies, listened to The Doors, unhinged, soaked about in thunderstorms. Clockwork-Oranging through stormwater felt like a calling—to me, it felt like a calling.

Never let anyone say one moment cannot, does not, alter all things.

I'm just not sure which one it was.

My other brother nearly died behind Wrigley Field. Three strangers, one baseball bat, trigonometry. But that wasn't the moment—it was the swell of moments after, each one a function of our most regrettable traits.

His and his and mine and theirs.

There are so many bits I am missing. If I'd taken a photo that night in Emergency, I would've only caught the blood on his head, but not on the fence, in the grass.

And not his voice—high above/(I was not)there—or how he vaulted over.

Death for the Idea

"Pshtt!" I cry, "You don't belong here. You are divisible."

The airplanes I daubed a mottled
blue. Made painted cloud. Overcast days
it was near impossible to make out what exactly
had come to bomb the city. I was told
they wouldn't bomb the cities, but the cities
were bombed. Pilots received directions
for panels, on how to fight, to remain
conscious. After three aces in error
toured ruins they'd flown over purposefully
losing mass, they begged for grounding.
The thing was: no one would let them stop
going up, nor the drops. And so the boys
(they were boys) decided to stop asking
no one. The first went AWOL and downed
himself on tracks of metro, the second looked
into barrel, found spiraling earth, the third
jumped. A swift river is not technically ground
but was conducive. They might've lingered here
in the world if there'd been no art involved.
Without knowledge or concept of consent
the trio'd been made pregnant then sent
to deliver children whose names were all
Death. But it is never facts. In truth

AUTOPORTRAIT (AS FLOTSAM)

it was a sublime camouflage proved
the upper wombs rotten—aluminum
I had painstakingly disguised as sky.

(Paul Klee)

The woods, crushed between cul-de-sacs.

I was twelve and there were bright new bones of house—sudden dozens of sapling skeletons—plotted up the block. Acres of jutting frame where a meadow had used to yawn, dandruffed with white butterflies and, beyond it, a wood sloping deerful down to the Conodoguinet.

The homes were see-through, trespassable, and we did.

We tried out a dry spigot and made a plan to return once things were plumbed—in sabotage.

That week we'd learned in the Johnstown Flood of 1889 more than 2,200 died. But we weren't conjuring bodies, their distorted bloat. No. We pictured gingham dresses adrift in damwater, tin cars silt-sunk, bicycles monstrous with algae. Romance.

In actuality, a whole town had piled up in matchsticks at a stone bridge, some of the flood-dead dead from fire. These unfleshed houses were like that : tinder.

Were we not our own Fates? Had we not scissors, left-handeds? Snip, snip. Powers of protection and destruction surged in us, motive. Dark wind in bony limb.

Pre-crones, we knew what we must.

That expanse of weedfield had kept us hid, intact, a prepubescent clutch of ferals down a snail of road curling past sewage plant toward the river. We must apply some element.

The cheerful-but-awful sign planted at the turn-off read : *Coming Soon—Victoria Glen*. But the only Glen we knew sold pot down at the park and rode a dirt bike.

We all did.

The Researchers

Perhaps it is like being shut in a cellar.

They say that but they don't know.
They are aboveground where sky is as
red as is nighttime. One might assume
they combed the shoreline on their bellies
attracting metals with shining bile. Coinage.
White worms like these ones are ever turning
into horseflies. They can't be ridden not one
inch forward or they buckle, throw the rider
into conniption. Faint grating sounds rise
from the sand, demons a-séance under-
sole. They can pierce the hallux or heel of
the waltzing dead among us to find new
bodies. We are what help them go on.
Once a blue moon the researchers notice
an artist or a writer infected, and they
must—they feel they *must*—act
the inquisitor. Real horror is
a clever grub, and climbs.

(Edvard Munch)

Joy is heavy machinery. Tumble within it, it will hang you over.
Everything in its wake covered in chalkdust, wet wool, fog.
Schooled, in its most anesthetizing sense.

Never assume.

I mean—*first there is a mountain*. A sleeping giant. Slowly
disappearing yet she persists. But the child-bride stalking across her
ridge as if free? That one is long gone, her cells poorly replicated
every handful of years.

Look at her here, a pile of painted rubies.

Over here, in cinderblock.

Her ashy shins, discarded hair; here, her tarot of swingsets.

She is nothing if not parabolic. I am nothing if knot. Desperate
for someone to untie her being—with their gaze. A thing we have
learned not to say.

Desire is as devastating as it is endless.

A Möbius ribbon snakes its wants between millennia. She, stripped
bare by her artifacts, even. Boots worn, Achilles jacked—it is a
long hike just to feel, or be

reminded : these are no mountains :: as I am

no real boy.

(Donovan)

Contingent

It is there as part of its anatomy.

When too much there is not here
either, escape transpires through the formal. Im-
precise repetitions. Breathing. There's a train runs amok
of the news, Haven and York, and on board
I can exist as neither girl, harp, woman
nor fiberglass. What happens
happens because of the way light twists
as it filters in. Celluloid's amber
turned flypaper. Never ride a train before noon
when its spiraling bullets make of passengers
rodents, skittering forth with gnawing
mouths in promulgation of the
illusion: progress.
                                        Evenings
when the light tangles around bodies loosely
in the compartment, and you've been gotten
wine from the café car, when all status
is in tantalizing question—you can
allow yourself to wax. Grow big by refusing
use. They will never know what not to do
with you. This is layering, a vanish into
potential, a technique to impossibilize
biography. My material they may long to have

illuminated. But I am no monk, no man-
uscript. And within this doubt
no woman you cannot.

(Eva Hesse)

After college I temped across Manhattan, tightroping overtime between skyscrapers until I had enough for a ticket.

In Paris in late March, sky and buildings fought a dovegray and off-white war, the low architecture invariably wearing its subtlety with more panache, churches interrupting. But I developed a fondness for the clouds amassing from fields like on a market day. Also d'Orsay, all arches and color and clocks.

Three weeks I stayed with my aunt and her husband outside the city as it bloomed—the path down to the RER along the Marne, the windowboxes, umbrellas, cemeteries.

They worked.

I'd ride into Paris in the morning, return for dinner: an omelet, or mussels in wine with day-old bread, arugula after.

One rained-out day I holed up in their apartment alone to watch the glitching VHS and cry. *Burning Secret, In the Heat of the Night, Lolita.* Windows open, curtains—a maroon shantung, wet and molding—the sill below my knees.

I thought to pray, discovered I could not.

I'd seen the black-and-white blonde actress, that she was far too old to be ruined, that it had *been* time I ruined myself.

III.

nomad
(star)

You will be released from your contract if your behavior is beyond the pale. If you only commit small murders you may be resurrected. You, but not them.

In July the crickets will sing. Just not the one you killed.

It is not July.

(A willow tosses itself into wind, you tripping under the Pleiades, those pitiless sisters.)

Sometime in the early aughts drones started making murder an arcade job. You could go to the war north of Vegas, your deaths meth dreams, and return to your family each night. BTK resurfaced then too, noising like cicada, his children grown. Yours just born.

Mine anyway.

I make these maps out of fog. Scratched with scattered branch, tree trash. Under stars so faint I'm forced to scrub the sky with salt to solve the light.

Untitled (Phrenology Box)

Maybe even the galaxy is holistic.

Then there's the split between
beauty and reality. There's the fault line
dividing them and threads that traverse it.
There are the large women with thunderbolt
needles and the smaller figures single-
filing it, ant-ish, across high voltage ropes.
There is the chasm and faces
haunting its waters in funhouse cut-out.
An ocean obliviates *and* it is mirror. A bed opens
into open field, its emptied bottles smashed
: sharp sheets of blue star. There's a feeling
—constriction at the heart of the throat
which is, you recall, the serpent first limbs con-
verged around. There's the wit some have
that we are passages. There's reasons
the objects must encounter me through windows
they make in themselves. There is that hard way
daughters have of choosing then reshaping
their mothers. There's voice. There's de-
formation. Sudden torque and the slow
undo before song is granted. And sometimes
knot. Twine. The divine is in fact all there
is, the debased—the humming between.

(Betye Saar)

Backstage, there was a smell. It smelled like a lack of time. Not not enough, not there at all.

We floated on quilts on concrete, nibbling goldfish, waiting for our class to be called out under the lights.

We wore makeup.

Our mothers were very serious about it, the hair, the ribbons on our shoes.

It was there I learned how to make every thing the most important thing.

Books, like people, when they reach their expiration dates, smell *off*. I was not pregnant yet, but the escalator down would frighten me when I became pregnant.

I feared feet I could not see might miss a step. How I missed them.

At five a.m. I came in to shelve the new titles and pull all the bindings to the front, equal as whores in a whore shop. This was called *facing* the books.

We were not allowed to read at work but I read at work.

Medical narratives were my favorite type of book I would never buy. I learned about female problems. There are so many female problems, I had no idea.

A longstanding medical misunderstanding of pleasure has been twinned historically with a grave misunderstanding of pain: a disbelief of their pain that puts women in graves.

While I worked at the bookshop, a friend of a friend, a heart surgeon, was diagnosed with breast cancer. The breast is anterior to the heart, for some, obscuring it.

For two years she insisted things were not right with her. Her colleagues disagreed. It was touch and go for a while. Eventually thick fingers of chemotherapy rummaged through her veins.

My coworkers at the bookshop found me illegible. I sometimes cried while facing, other times while destroying, books. To them—these were different acts.

But pregnancy was what happened because I was feeling deeply, not vice versa.

Between games and religion I discovered my child's name. It means "to witness from above." This was not the child I conceived that year: he is a different one, we all are. Different books.

Wait long enough and we rot. We become genreless, dead, too old to carry meaning or children. We are pulped. We are books and books are over. In the future, only certain women will read them, and then only to one another in the depths of night when the malls have closed for good and the internet failed.

Given enough time, our skin will begin to glow as if lit by blood or phosphorescent fetus.

As we read, we may sigh backwards, into how any poor thing comes to be—through careless love, or happenstance, or neglect. A summer night, for example, beside a lake in sepsis, heavy metal deranging the nymphs. Ephemeroptera.

Our gradual descent into the future is a species of pleasure I call *untoward*, which—the way I say it—sounds like *untoed*. (My own feet were returned to me after each childbirth, intact.)

Most things I think deserve a name.

Mooring

You are living and I keep you in one still piece alive.

On the ice, everything held quiet, and after—
marks from knives we wore on our feet.
It takes practice, living cold. I was convinced
a partner was needed to survive it. I scuttled
blood into blue territory for later extraction.
It isn't as if we won't die. Poet and sister. Equinox.
Our parents scarce need mentioning, legend
before our first rebellions sifted to earth in leaves
felled. Thin arms were an aesthetic choice, small
heads like ova, nodding between the immensity
of an independent life or a return to Chicago.
Wide streets we called boulevards. Skies stretched
out of reach, then elevators. Somewhere else
a mechanical piano tiredly lifted its hands to etch
frost into rust. Berceuse. Landscaped, you I held
faster than winter, in seizure. *Vivant sans merci.*

(Joan Mitchell)

My father and mother are jointly writing a book of their lives. He wants to record what *of* him is still *with* him. She would prefer not to.

She says so sometimes, on the phone.

But also he is remembering less (though sometimes small details arrive in his mind with strength and will not leave, she tells me). She is putting asterisks beside any material she does not understand his logic for. Ticks on the page I'll want to smash but won't.

This is a book of both.

Over-articulation of the trivial is a hallmark. As if it fills the absences—fixing things. No, no... we did not pass through Frederick, it was Fredericks*berg*. Things like this.

One day, I may edit their lives. She says she will pay me, as if one accepts money for such efforts, and of course one does. If one is such a one. But I was born second and became third. Electrified like a rail in the underground. I will not accept.

My father joked long ago about naming me Elektra. It's funny, if you know the Sophocles. Sad, if you've heard of the grieving star become a comet.

I wish they were more comfortable, my parents, with sprawl. I like order too. Every sentence, a toothpick sculpture. A miniature craft set on the water like a drama. Where will I end? The Land of Toys, where lazy boys become donkeys, irrevocably—at least in the Disney. In the *Odyssey* it was swine and reversible. It was not, for an example, a metaphor for aging.

I have three boys. Had. They are not mine, you do not mine children.

I won't.

I once assumed gender differentiated personality. Not really a thing.

I fell in love with curiosity, but science is unrewarding of mistake (exception: Alexander Fleming, a man.) Nor does an aesthetics garner respect (see: Sally Mann, woman). And children? Wayward wards. Leeward, backwards, backwoods, woodbine. Climbers and creepers and clingers—until not.

The holes in me where their tendrils once hooked now teem with other worms, ones our symbiosis briefly held at bay.

Bay is a word for waiting room. Harbor for safety. Rivers mean home and oceans death and children not-afraid.

Of sloshing over, melding flood and tentacle in some strange lovecraft. Forgive.

And this whole time unmothers are asked (by whom exactly?) to mince around with small cloths. Or knives made of camera. To dab away any excess escaped them through swamps of blood, mucus, and shit. Or isolate it. (Photograph, penicillin.)

They are a kind of melt, children. Bits of the glacial unmother

sloughing off—to watch you slip like ice—glinting oceans of self
and death. Control it, quick.

Use ink.

(Lucille Clifton)

The Crossing

Later, whenever I sketched, it was on the sly.

They let you do it, when you exist
in alone the sky.
Aether things are not the same
amount restricted. Not until I was lifted
from hotspring as some thing
beyond this bloody coil
did creation accept me as potential
material. Firmament. At once
I had talent. Ghosts aren't what you think
before you become very thin. I style
words on fog on mirrors. I trace shapes
on faces on the sleeping. Half-smile chevrons
of ghostknife—monalisal. This is
how portraitists lose their heads. On snow
I've scrawled latenight notes of trans-
lucence describing the way light
arrives solely through latticework.
With what I am no longer I renounce
my limbs, their peripheral fingers
sieves. To draw breath—I have learned
merely dilutes the art with a willful
and a reckless incorporation.

(Romaine Brooks)

Ode to a Shroud/Smock—

over its ghost-tent folds, charcoal smudge of stick-figured lives
dancing/in mock of the one I don't lead, can't describe how/I
trail behind—how there-I-am! running after the organ-grinder
of it/so far ahead of me I never catch the girl/she happens
beyond my wit

loose episodes strung together with laundry line, tightrope,
thread/of a pencil and she, me, a marionette tying our hands/in
cradles, distracted by piano/inside a museum of was

shoebox panorama: Chagall to paint the backdrop/even dead,
his colors linger within/the dark—all I have ever known

: ekphrasis begins with an urn

At twenty I canoed up the Swatara with a man I did not know at all, very well, for seven years. Time enough my cells replaced themselves with doppelgängers. Hours fighting current only to acquiesce in drift.

That night I think we played Scrabble.

I have been told at the beginning my voice got soft when he called, the telephone attached to the wall, me in the kitchen, my family around the corner and no door. He wrote a letter when I left, mailed it to my grad school, I remember it was lovely, printed on parchment-colored resumé paper, the kind with a watermark.

There was a magazine store I asked to be taken to as a child, the next town over. My father would buy Sunday *Times* and Salem Lights. I'd select from a long drawer single lilac pages that felt like cloth.

I'd get halfway through the crossword. Drop it.

During college summers I taught middle-schoolers books. We took fieldtrips. The crew on a restored schooner showed us what sailing was—how to tie down, avoid the boom, breathe. People used to vanish on the sea, but we were reading sci-fi.

Stars, solar wind, hard labor, pale horizon.

The program was paid for by my university. My students and I could not have otherwise afforded the water.

AUTOPORTRAIT (AS FLOTSAM)

In revision I traveled inland, every landscape a new stanza. There are oceans too of pewter wheat. Decades after Iowa, high above the town of Stepantsminda, I felt as if I might once again set out over the edge of the world, my black dress billowing :

in a sea of cresting mountains I saw how everything can happen

:: to use all seven letters—I should—all at once.

Synopsis of a Battle

I didn't have to bother with myself ever, except as a vehicle...

A Mustang, Pontiac. These are names from Dorothy's West, a place
fewer live because they are for dogs—prairies. People, fielding in the minor
league, they like a tree. During a war, a copse invites retreat. I treat
color as primary. Blood is red and grass, green. Most of us need oxygen
to glow. I'm not a patient man. Facts gloat thru history's fishbowl, claiming
space, denying angle. A shaft of light can make a halo—and behind me?
Soldiers gather. I remove them from the board. I bang erasers until my sons
choke on the chalk. That, or ask for a baseball. I am a liar. Any person
at almost any time can art. Can fuck an artist. Everything needed to
fight gods is culled from the pitcher's release: ropey neck pulling away
from projectile, the in-turn of the following leg. These form an index.
A brick road. To grapple with a mountain over which armies have fled
I've found grottos helpful. Wax figures. Whatever passes I fold into a kind
of Christ. No fastball. My seed-sorrow was I could not throw. Big though
they are as stadium, my canvases whisper—toss, toy, make vague to catch.

(Cy Twombly)

We moved through dropped kindling of ghosttrees and tree-
choking vines to reach the clearing, an enormous field of tall grass
humming caught sun in the growing dark.

A picnic blanket spread before us cokes and watermelon. Did I sit?

I was five. I cartwheeled. My red handkerchief dress—an upside-
rightside-down poppy, a rolling cola can-can.

Fireworks tipped out of a star bucket onto a silhouette jutting
skyward the adolescent shoulders and hips of rollercoaster, an
empty pie-faced wheel. The far side of amusement.

Explosions at a distance.

And what was I? At home there not at all in the center of things.
Deeply at home in a place I'd never been before nor would again
(uncounting now), etching the small script of my body into twilit
margin. Since my first pass through thicket—I've been charmed

by mere suggestion of headlight, astigmatic star.

Are baseball fields lodged along the tracks so bored sisters can court death? (Pennies on the rail.)

After I did not die of defiant fibroid, the geneticist suggested we take Amtrak from Baltimore to Seattle and halfway back. Baseball diamonds, warehouses, dogs, deer, mountains, backyard appliances, a green river through magenta redbuds.

Sleeping semi-upright is a skill.

I spent days staring at the spring that was not there until California, that disappeared again in Montana.

Spring is a volume of time not defined by month but by breeds of color. The greens, lilac. Mars I think has no spring. Nor the moon.

Years before we'd visited Finland where April is defined by thaw, silver-white replaced by long days, shades of wren. Low sun extending lakes in an unvanishing.

In Kentucky and again in Oregon I wondered if some trash was hoarded for color. So that when the snow retreated, things would immediately begin to sing.

Winterbirds manage joy all winter long, questing among rust and plastic toys for errant seed. The promise—*green will follow.*

Along the summer tracks, Empress trees shoot up in vertical lilypad, ladders to some moon where the rain's gone sideways. As it does in a landscape passed through.

All this seeking, and we end up traveling like Lincoln in his box.

Without uteri. Faces smashed up against the country.

Hotel Bedroom

I'm only trying to do what I can't do.

I can't do listening, not like I am
supposed. I get too caught up in the colors
of skin. They talk to me and the more
they do the less patience I've
with vowels. Ooo. Nothing lives sub-word
though there is a wild and pulsating
mass of preserves in the body, barely and I mean
barely contained by membranes. Also—
in certain countries where I've had the bad
luck of study or holiday—there are whole
dark colleges aimed at anatomizing
architecture. The conjecture : beams and struts
are bone. But this is lies. Organism.
Buildings are clinical, inert. Every last one
an asylum, platelets thickening in stagnant corridors
as refugees will. The thing a body wants
is to be starfished. To turn upon itself, dead
rhymes replaced with sheen
of freed viscera. But like a pullover
thrown over arm-chair-back, the body
also wants—more than anything else
it wants—a snuffing out. To be touristed
: its very shed forgot in the offing.

(Lucian Freud)

I once dreamt a swingset made of metal, a contraption monstrous as a scoliotic brace.

But, also, on it I could push myself with arms not legs, an industrial-type pump—as if we children were all of us water-hoarders, training to drain dry the deepest well. Or all that is well and good.

Weeks later I visited cousins and, with them, followed a shaggy runnel through a ravine to a deep park with pines, and the beast I dreamt is there, and I tell no one.

Prophecy is a fickle business.

Even at that raw age, I knew people untrusted truths not manufactured by their own machines.

I first met Louise Bourgeois's drawings in a book, though she is known as a sculptor.

I read what she said about art that was not her *main* art:

These are maggots. It looks like a very negative subject. In fact, it is not a negative subject at all. In fact, if I were religious, I would say that it is the theme of the resurrection.

In a single body, there hide any number of childhoods. Maturity I think is a myth—and time, an illusion made impossible to treat as illusion by aging.

The containment of our bodies in space creates the fantasy of space.

Our bodies' housing of other bodies (fetuses and tumors alike) fosters still other delusions: immortality, cessation.

Bourgeois knew this. She redrew the same line drawings over decades.

A famous installation of her architectural sculptures at the Tate Modern was titled *I do, I undo, I redo.*
Spirals, enormous staircase, tiny shell—these say time and growth do not move as they are perceived to.

Maggots know this. Crows, also.

Roof Song

I am a map. You are a different map.

From here the windows are sharp and truly
that's all one needs. When I cut myself
shaving in the bath I think *blood, as it tries
to be smoke.* One asks for a long
attrition, relevance, to stay on top of
life because the alternative
is crepuscular. Light draining unbearably away
the arbitrary
                    until world feels stark
and meant. The mass of things pulls
against logic. Americans remain convinced
they are as they planned they'd be
spilling lilac knocks of hardened prose
which I suppose only human, a quality
I've never much admired. And so
the soft-edged fissures of childhood
get wallpapered over
and over. Maché. Replay a film
enough times
                    and nebulae form. Light—
that star-souvenir—once had a body and now
nothing does. It would be too facile
to weave this late mind into a tapestry of tells
but it is a thing I could do. Become

binary. Blinking once : *you-can't-get-*
there-from-here.
Twice for *vrai.*

(Louise Bourgeois)

It's so hard. The hearse itself prompting me.

Not a particular vehicle, else a civil carriage. A fleet of queer horses and snow. You think of things you tried to let go and all of them are churches.

A sighting of a woman in a white dress down by the creek, the photograph echoed : a 1920s bridesmaid with crossed ankles and pearl-buttoned shoes. How it lived on my parents' bookshelf for a decade, two flights above the encyclopedia. How utterly certain I am of this fact.

No one else recalls her.

I am nearly dead—if not in terms of corpse, there are other terms. My parents, though, are so close to the actual event that it may behoove me to wait. The unlikeliest daughter.

I should maybe not. Fuck. Not speak of unpleasant things until they merit swearing. Then—go at it like a sailor.

When he was a child my father was in the navy. In which capacity he failed to reach the war.

This is one way things can go : on.

It's too late for loving on grammar, everyone saying to not. But things we don't leave marks. Splintering boats towed to pasture. They go, I go, echo. The declining.

When he called his mother from port, clip-clop, her silence
dropped harder than his f-bomb. She died soon after his discharge.
He was not two past twenty.

It must be her I've often thought—in the picture, her eyes patent—
with the shoes.

I grew up in beauty, a word worn to nub from overuse. How the Appalachians have been made less sublime over eons, more passable. There's a trail.

Hand to hand, coins lose their faces.

I got married on the Susquehanna, a railroad bridge and a small stretch of the Blue Mountain over my shoulder—the veil the world, its train longing.

I could not live with beauty, I am not her wife.

Here's the thing. I tied myself to four. Buoys all. There's also the tug of water.

Some nomads move through deserts, places they cannot tolerate or places they will not long be tolerated. I think they are the most sane, living off what is there and leaving when what is there is not.

I did not marry a nomad nor have I flushed any from my womb. I don't think.

Still—I wander.

Others have memory and they are luckier.

Swan Lake #2

The landscapes were in my arms as I did it.

Where else would they hide themselves? They were too
large, too smokeful to curl within the digital, depleted
realm. They were more than their piney scent, tucked into
forests of the armpit. I carried them as one carries
firewood, children. All kinds of kindling. And then
I set fire to them. That is how you make it all
happen at once—you create a conflagration. It is obvious.
It has to be obvious. When you murder your small ones
there is no funeral, just sooty plots polka-dotting the yard
like you've sown some chaotic vegetable. But you kill
an entire vista—you put the sublime to death by
committing to it—the body is involved. I used to think
the body was my body, that I was a thing making other
things. That was limited. Arms can only hold so much
beauty before corruption. Bones dislocate and the worlds
within disperse as if all that's wrought belongs to the
Earth. This inverts the illusions of men (oh, indeed
I have engaged): centrality first among them—first-
ness second. I wanted all of everything to happen
at once. That's why I spent years negotiating acts
of conversion. A pulsating architecture of ocean
conceived as dancehall : the dancehall, set on fire.

(Helen Frankenthaler)

Now they are gone and I look around and I think, *I was not built for them.*

I was wood.

But wood can be shaped—hewn into canoe or chapel, torch, puppet.

Or, approximately, mother.

When I couldn't sleep, still often, I would sit in the doorway of my parents' bedroom, locked onto the red digits of the alarm clock. Sometimes I'd wait an hour or more, balled up under a tent of flannel, a shiver in the narrow hall.

Again and again I tried to predict the moment forms would shift.

Between birth contractions, and during them—time changes character. Varying the lengths I was assured were identical, seconds turned on me.

I never thought their acrobatics malevolence.

Have I ever been the same?

The Spoonful of Milk

One cannot be precise and still be true.

How many times have I taken the wooden doll off
the shelf to let you play with it, child? But only
when I am there to watch. This doll
is a special doll, a painter's doll propped up
with a dowel's external spine, balls for
joints, and no categorical face. When you fly
her over the city of your toys I laugh. People rarely
fly. When you have the doll talk to your animals
I shake in silence, trying not to tell you
how cow and horse have no feeling
for human language. Their own is a cloven thing
they speak only at night in the dark
of the barn—a series of stomps punctuated
by gaunt and lifted necks—small lows
and whinnies below our hearing. I've caught them
passing knowing looks when I've arrived
blurry in the before-dawn, the hot milk steaming
fat, the color of the blackest horse a rich blue.
Like a furnace his coat shines and he knows
he is a god, and his face—the face of a god.
And this is why we leave the doll unpainted, child.

(Marc Chagall)

My siblings and I once plotted our escape on a spaceshipped bedspread: lines of egress between bedroom planets, the comet-path stairway, oxygenless plans B and C should we be discovered by the enemy.

Down below a dinner party convulsed—one to which we were not invited, one for whom we did not wish to perform.

Early evening knifed through the window fan. Long light sliced to petal.

The house a half-double, its *World Book* for arguments, deep carpet of green shag. Somewhere below our feet they laughed and that was guillotines, us cut off from their arch-and-clinking lower-mid suburban world.

I admit, it felt a type of freedom.

If we could slip past them and reach the slant of sideyard, where a few rosebushes flaunted cruel small thorns but little else lay in wait, our collapse into wet grass would let us know—

we'd no need of being held by anyone save gravity.

Recently I've lived in places Poe toasted his death while conjugating wrongly. Amo, amiss, amort. Of course he may not have. He did marry his cousin when she was thirteen—a fact not in dispute.

Apocryphal comforts.

Children should be taught that life is a play watched by callous angels. That there be monsters.

I cannot but transcend and -gress. Mend and guess. Bend and bless.

I have a goddaughter with a moon name. She is not my charge, but I claim some connection to her underground electricity, its inky spark surfaced as bruise. I don't flirt well with children, but I recognize in their pre-fledged souls something coming.

Something could.

I was that kind of child: arrhythmic, a drinker of dregs from glasses I'd dutifully cleared from the table. Raring to fight the dark where it erupts. Just there—a blueness bloomed sub-skin, negative wingspan, the heart wished hushed.

(Hush now.)

Time to stop beating against yourself/we shall have no more applause.

Atropos

The sleep of reason produces monsters.

Neither conception nor pregnancy
forms children. Birth is the actual if
tacit factory. Only as they are borne
down the ribbon of the intestines
do babies acquire feet and buttons.
In time, natty boots—added—can
offer both a fit home. The un-
bloodied buttons, safely transported
intact in infant stomachs, will one day
seek disgorging. Attachment. Want
to be fastened. And the sour white
of newborn spittle? That smells of
bone, because. The buttons are bone.

(Francisco Goya)

The few times I took the boys to the ocean, I tried to explain.

"This is where we end." What I meant was that it is lower than the mountains, that there are some of us seek bottom.

In the waves, we were lifted then dropped onto new sand, which is old shell. All the discarded homes ground to innumerable finities. The transformation feelable. The more a fragment is lessened, the softer on the sole, the palm of the foot.

The future, finer. Meager.

I walk to the harbor nearly daily to watch the gentle lapping resettle life below. The water clear and dark at once.

Clouds migrating above and upon, wound to scar to thief.

Desire pulls (us/them) apart like cirrus with only art to mark the shapes we've made against the sky. Despite the sky. To spite the gods whose names replace themselves like seasons, whose children bear faint imprint of the original conceit.

Because we cannot not, we remake—memory the matter

: flotsam.

There. I've done it, rid myself
(wooden tiles shed from
wooden boy) all seven

and we'll watch them fall.

All at once, the lettered clatter.

How oceansky gives birth over and over to rhyme until neither mother nor child knows the face of the other. This is the nature of the unmother : to lose count. Or, to try to make of the dying, sense.

At least—it is as I am.

How I would.

(the artist/once known)